BRINGING BACK THE

Humpback Whale

Kelly Spence

CRABTREE
PUBLISHING COMPANY
WWW.CRABTREEBOOKS.COM

CRABTREE
PUBLISHING COMPANY
WWW.CRABTREEBOOKS.COM

Author: Kelly Spence

Series Research and Development: Reagan Miller

Managing Editor: Tim Cooke

Picture Manager: Sophie Mortimer

Design Manager: Keith Davis

Editorial Director: Lindsey Lowe

Children's Publisher: Anne O'Daly

Editor: Janine Deschenes

Proofreader: Lorna Notsch

Cover design: Margaret Amy Salter

Production coordinator and
   Prepress technician: Margaret Amy Salter

Print coordinator: Katherine Berti

Produced for Crabtree Publishing Company
by Brown Bear Books

Photographs (t=top, b= bottom, l=left, r=right, c=center)

Front Cover: All images from Shutterstock

Interior: Alamy: Kelvin Aitkin/VWPics, 27t, Eric Carr, 11b, NOAA, 26, redbrickstock.com, 27c, SOTK2011, 9b, Jeremy Sutton-Hibbert, 15b, WaterFrame, 16; Getty Images: Barcroft Media, 18, Richard Olsenius/National Geographic, 15t, Photofusion/UIG, 13; iStock: duncan1890, 5b, miblue5, 1, PEDRE, 21, shauni, 19, Paul Wolf, 4; Library of Congress: 9t; Nature Picture Library: John Cancalosi, 6; NOAA: 7, 28, MMHSRP permit 923-1489, 20, Craig Smith/University of Hawaii, 11t; Shutterstock: Ethan Daniels, 29, Tomas Kotouc, 12, Robert Mcgillivray, 24, NaniP, 22-23, Vadim Petrakov, 14, Bram Reusen, 23, Michael Smith/ITWP, 5t, Dai Mar Tamarack, 10, John Tunney, 8.

Brown Bear Books has made every attempt to contact the copyright holder. If you have any information please contact licensing@brownbearbooks.co.uk

Library and Archives Canada Cataloguing in Publication

Spence, Kelly, author
      Bringing back the humpback whale / Kelly Spence.

(Animals back from the brink)
Includes index.
Issued in print and electronic formats.
ISBN 978-0-7787-4905-9 (hardcover).--
ISBN 978-0-7787-4938-7 (softcover).--
ISBN 978-1-4271-2105-9 (HTML)

      1. Humpback whale--Juvenile literature. 2. Humpback whale--Conservation--Juvenile literature. 3. Endangered species--Juvenile literature. 4. Wildlife recovery--Juvenile literature. I. Title.

QL737.C424S64 2018   j333.95'952516   C2018-903053-4
                                                                          C2018-903054-2

Library of Congress Cataloging-in-Publication Data

Names: Spence, Kelly, author.
Title: Bringing back the humpback whale / Kelly Spence.
Description: New York, New York : Crabtree Publishing, [2019] |
   Series: Animals back from the brink | Includes index.
Identifiers: LCCN 2018036872 (print) | LCCN 2018037482 (ebook) |
   ISBN 9781427121059 (Electronic) |
   ISBN 9780778749059 (hardcover : alk. paper) |
   ISBN 9780778749387 (paperback : alk. paper)
Subjects: LCSH: Humpback whale--Conservation--Juvenile literature.
Classification: LCC QL737.C424 (ebook) |
   LCC QL737.C424 S698 2019 (print) | DDC 599.5/25--dc23
LC record available at https://lccn.loc.gov/2018036872

Crabtree Publishing Company

www.crabtreebooks.com   1-800-387-7650

Printed in the U.S.A./102018/CG20180810

Published in Canada
Crabtree Publishing
616 Welland Ave.
St. Catharines, Ontario
L2M 5V6

Published in the United States
Crabtree Publishing
PMB 59051
350 Fifth Avenue, 59th Floor
New York, New York 10118

Published in the United Kingdom
Crabtree Publishing
Maritime House
Basin Road North, Hove
BN41 1WR

Published in Australia
Crabtree Publishing
3 Charles Street
Coburg North
VIC, 3058

Contents

Find videos and extra material online at **crabtreeplus.com** to learn more about the conservation of animals and ecosystems. See page 30 in this book for the access code to this material.

The Edge of Extinction

Humpback whales are some of the largest animals on Earth. They can grow to almost 63 feet (19 meters) in length and weigh up to 40 tons (36 metric tonnes). Humpbacks are found in all the world's oceans. They spend the summer feeding in cold waters, but travel great distances to warmer areas to **breed** and raise their young. At one time, these massive **mammals** existed in large numbers. They do not have many natural **predators**. However, from the 1600s onward, humans became their biggest threat with the rise of the whaling **industry**.

Despite their massive size, humpbacks are famous for their **acrobatic** movements. They slap and wave their long fins on the ocean surface. They use their powerful tail fin, called a fluke, to leap out of the water. This is called breaching.

Humpback whales do not reproduce, or have babies, quickly. Individuals start to **mate** around the age of seven. A female carries her baby for about a year. After birth, the baby whale stays with its mother for another year. A female gives birth every two to four years.

HUNTED TO NEAR EXTINCTION

During the 1600s, whaling, or whale hunting, developed in Europe. Whalers hunted different species for oil, meat, and **blubber**. The demand for oil grew because it was a popular type of fuel used to power machines. At first, whalers hunted humpbacks in their local areas. But as whale populations dropped, whalers began to journey farther out to sea. Faster boats allowed them to chase down the slow-swimming mammals. More powerful and effective weapons were developed, and more humpbacks were hunted. The worldwide whale population quickly dropped. By the mid-1900s, humpbacks and many other species of whales were on the brink of **extinction**.

Species at Risk

Created in 1984, the International Union for the **Conservation** of Nature (IUCN) protects wildlife, plants, and **natural resources** around the world. Its members include about 1,400 governments and nongovernmental organizations. The IUCN publishes the Red List of Threatened **Species** each year, which tells people how likely a plant or animal species is to become **extinct**. It began publishing the list in 1964.

SCIENTIFIC CRITERIA

The Red List, created by scientists, divides nearly 80,000 species of plants and animals into nine categories. Criteria for each category include the growth and **decline** of the population size of a species. They also include how many individuals within a species can breed, or have babies. In addition scientists include information about the habitat of the species, such as its size and quality. These criteria allow scientists to figure out the probability of extinction facing the species.

The ivory-billed woodpecker of the southeastern United States has been listed as Critically Endangered (CR) since 2000. The IUCN updates the Red List twice a year to track the changing of species. Each individual species is reevaluated at least every five years.

IUCN LEVELS OF THREAT

The Red List uses nine categories to define the threat to a species.

Extinct (EX)	No living individuals survive
Extinct in the Wild (EW)	Species cannot be found in its natural habitat. Exists only in **captivity**, in **cultivation**, or in an area that is not its natural habitat.
Critically Endangered (CR)	At extremely high risk of becoming extinct in the wild
Endangered (EN)	At very high risk of extinction in the wild
Vulnerable (VU)	At high risk of extinction in the wild
Near Threatened (NT)	Likely to become threatened in the near future
Least Concern (LC)	Widespread, abundant, or at low risk
Data Deficient (DD)	Not enough data to make a judgment about the species
Not Evaluated (NE)	Not yet evaluated against the criteria

In the United States, the Endangered Species Act of 1973 was passed to protect species from possible extinction. It has its own criteria for classifying species, but they are similar to those of the IUCN. Canada introduced the Species at Risk Act in 2002. More than 530 species are protected under the act. The list of species is compiled by the Committee on the Status of Endangered Wildlife in Canada (COSEWIC).

HUMPBACK WHALES AT RISK

In 1973, humpback whales were listed as Endangered under the U.S. Endangered Species Act (ESA). The IUCN Red List classified the humpback whale as Endangered in 1986 and Vulnerable in 1990, but in 2008, it was reclassified as being of Least Concern. In 2016, the global humpback population was divided into 14 distinct population segments (DPS) under the Endangered Species Act. Today, the ESA lists four DPS of humpbacks as being Endangered and one as Near Threatened.

Humpbacks under Threat

Indigenous peoples have hunted humpbacks for thousands of years. They only hunt what they need, so whale populations are not dramatically affected. This is called **subsistence** whaling. Europeans began hunting whales during the Middle Ages (500–1500 C.E.). They hunted many types of whales, including humpbacks. When whales became less plentiful near Europe, whalers began traveling farther out to sea. In the 1800s, the whaling industry expanded in North America. Boats traveled to hunt whales in the Arctic and Antarctica. The numbers of all whales fell. New Bedford, Massachusetts, was a whaling port on the East Coast of the United States. In the 1840s, about 400 whaling vessels operated there. In 1850, New Bedford was the wealthiest city in the United States.

BALEEN

TONGUE

Baleen is a strong, flexible material that hangs inside a humpback's mouth. In the 1700s and 1800s, it was in demand to make items such as **corsets** and whips.

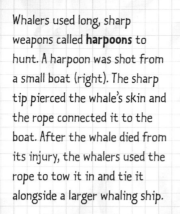

Whalers used long, sharp weapons called **harpoons** to hunt. A harpoon was shot from a small boat (right). The sharp tip pierced the whale's skin and the rope connected it to the boat. After the whale died from its injury, the whalers used the rope to tow it in and tie it alongside a larger whaling ship.

OVERHUNTING

By the 1900s, whaling took place in several countries, including Canada. In the early to mid-1900s, about 220,000 humpbacks were killed in the Southern **Hemisphere** alone. At this time, more reliable fuel sources became more popular than whale oil, and demand for whale oil fell. But the damage was done. Humpbacks and other whales had been hunted to the edge of existence. By 1966, there were only about 1,400 humpbacks left in the world's oceans.

A dead whale waits to be processed at a whaling station, or processing plant, on Vancouver Island in British Columbia, Canada, in 1926.

Ecosystem Engineers

There is still much scientists do not know about humpbacks, but we have started to recognize the important role whales such as humpbacks play in ocean **ecosystems**. Humpbacks are near the top of the **food chain**, which means they have no natural predators. Although sometimes orcas and sharks attack humpbacks, it is not common. Disrupting one part of an ecosystem's food chain affects its other species, too. As a top predator in the food chain, humpbacks help keep populations of **krill** under control. As krill eat a living thing called plankton, this leaves more plankton for other species to eat.

Humpbacks feed mainly on krill and small fish. Each whale eats between 1–1.5 tons (0.9–1.4 metric tonnes) of food each day. Humpbacks sometimes work together to blow bubbles to trap krill. This is called bubble netting.

WHALE FALL

When a humpback dies, its body sometimes sinks to the **ocean floor**. This is called a whale fall. Whale falls play an important role in an ocean ecosystem. Animals such as sharks, crabs, and fish feed off the whale's **tissue**. This helps break down the remains into **nutrients** that feed invertebrates (animals without backbones), such as snails and worms.

Invertebrates also settle on the whale skeleton (right). Some researchers believe whale hunting disrupted this natural cycle. The nutrients were no longer available as a food source for invertebrates, and could have caused the extinction of many deep-water species that humans had not yet discovered.

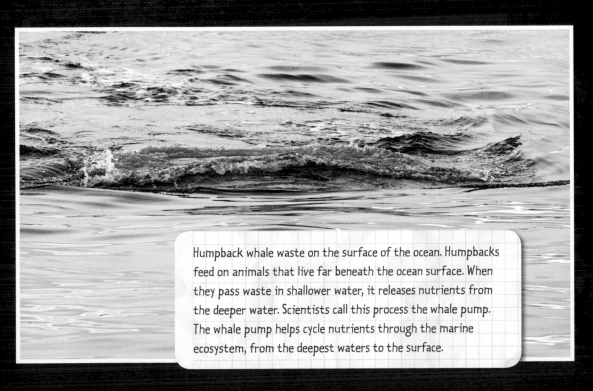

Humpback whale waste on the surface of the ocean. Humpbacks feed on animals that live far beneath the ocean surface. When they pass waste in shallower water, it releases nutrients from the deeper water. Scientists call this process the whale pump. The whale pump helps cycle nutrients through the marine ecosystem, from the deepest waters to the surface.

Saving the Whales

The International Whaling Commission (IWC) was founded in 1946. Its goal was to make sure that there were enough whales to hunt for money. As whale numbers fell, it began trying to protect the remaining whales. In 1955, the IWC banned hunting humpbacks in the North Atlantic. In 1964, a ban was applied to the Southern Hemisphere. In 1966, hunting of humpbacks was banned completely. The IWC takes countries that illegally break the bans to court. In 2018, the IWC had 87 member countries, including the United States.

Canada was a founding member of the IWC. However, in 1981, the country withdrew because it no longer has a whaling industry.

WHALE SONG RAISES AWARENESS

Today, humpbacks are well-known for the unique sounds they make. The repeating patterns of chirps and moans made by humpbacks are songlike. These sounds were first recorded in the late 1960s by Scott McVay, who shared his findings with a fellow **biologist** named Roger Payne. Payne played the recordings to a singer named Judy Collins. In 1970, Collins released an album called *Whales & Nightingales* that included humpbacks singing in the background of a song. The album introduced many people to the humpback—and made them aware of the movement to save the whales. Part of the profits from the album went to conservation efforts.

COLLABORATING FOR A CAUSE

Greenpeace is an international organization that works to conserve the environment. It was founded in 1971. During the 1970s and 1980s, the organization began fighting to end whaling by making countries obey the whaling bans. Its famous motto was "Save the whales!" By 1973, **activists** began to follow whaling vessels from countries such as Japan and the Soviet Union that broke the IWC whaling bans. They tried to stop the hunts by driving small boats in the way of the whalers' harpoons, so they could not shoot the whales (right). By doing so, they placed pressure on the IWC to enforce the whaling bans more effectively.

Putting a Plan into Action

In 1982, the IWC announced a **moratorium** on whaling for business. The ban came into effect in 1986 and made it illegal to hunt any whales for money. The plan was to allow humpbacks to breed safely, so the population would grow. However, the IWC has little power. It relies on its members to enforce the ban. This allows countries such as Japan to break the ban relatively easily. Many countries have their own plans to protect whales. In the United States, the Marine Mammal Protection Act (MMPA) protects all marine animals in U.S. waters. In Canada, the Department of Fisheries and Oceans (DFO) protects humpback populations in the North Atlantic and North Pacific.

There are a few exceptions to the hunting ban. The **Inuit** in Greenland are allowed to continue with subsistence whaling. So can the population of Saint Vincent and the Grenadines (SVG), a small country in the Caribbean. Under the IWC, SVG can hunt up to four humpbacks a year for food, clothing, and fuel.

The Inuit have hunted humpback whales for more than 4,000 years. In 2010, the IWC gave Greenland Inuit permission to hunt a total of 27 humpbacks over three years. However, the wildlife charity Whale and Dolphin Conservation (WDC) reported that more whales were caught illegally. Their meat was being sold, rather than being used as a traditional food by the Inuit.

STILL AT RISK

Countries such as Japan, Norway, and Iceland argue that whale populations, including the humpback, have recovered enough to allow for whaling. In 2007, Japan announced that it would hunt 50 humpback whales as part of a scientific program to learn about whales (right). However, there are other ways to study whales without killing them. Conservation groups expressed concern. Japan still claims a right to hunt these animals. In 2016, fishers in Norway said they should be free to hunt whales, including humpbacks. They argued that whales eat too many fish and damage fishers' livelihoods. Many scientists do not agree that this is true.

Back from the Brink

The hunting bans and protection efforts were effective. In 2008, the IUCN officially changed the status of humpbacks from Vulnerable to Least Concern. The decision was based on a steadily increasing number of humpbacks. However, the IUCN noted vulnerable populations living in the Arabian Sea, the western North Pacific, off the west coast of Africa, and in the South Pacific near Oceania (between Asia and North and South America). The United States and Canada also changed the status of the humpbacks as their numbers grew. In 2011, COSEWIC raised the status of humpbacks in the North Pacific and North Atlantic, but it said that both groups still needed to be watched carefully to ensure that their numbers did not fall again.

The most recent global population of humpback whales was estimated at more than 60,000. Although the number of humpbacks is increasing in many places, it is still important to protect these animals to make sure these populations do not decline again.

COLLABORATING FOR A CAUSE

The smallest humpback population lives in the Arabian Sea, in the northern Indian Ocean. The Arabian Sea Whale Network (ASWN) is a group of organizations that collaborate to protect this population. Researchers photograph the animals so that they can be identified and tracked as they move. They also attach tags to whales to enable identification and monitoring. Scientists use these methods to learn about the whales' breeding habits and the health of the population.

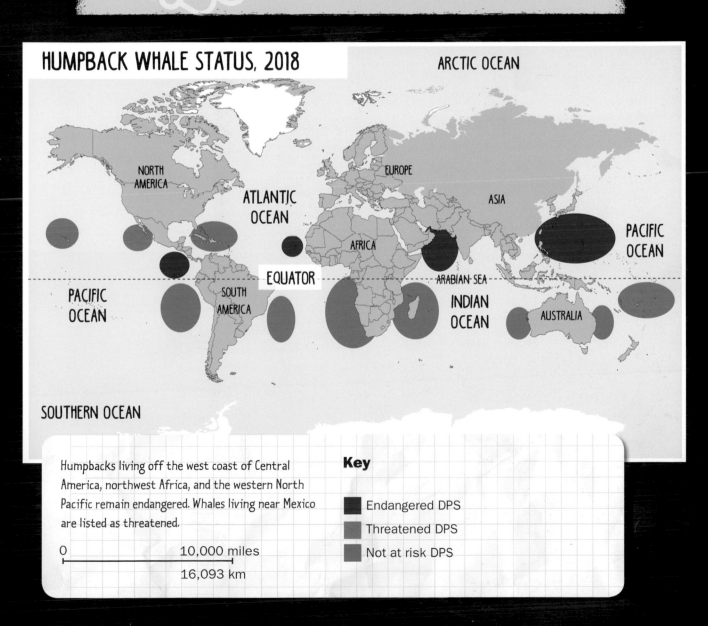

HUMPBACK WHALE STATUS, 2018

Humpbacks living off the west coast of Central America, northwest Africa, and the western North Pacific remain endangered. Whales living near Mexico are listed as threatened.

0   10,000 miles

16,093 km

Key

- Endangered DPS
- Threatened DPS
- Not at risk DPS

Continuing Threats

Despite the bans on whale hunting, the humpback still faces dangers. Entanglement is when a marine animal gets tangled in gear being used by fishers. For example, fishers drop traps to the ocean floor to catch lobsters. The traps have long ropes that attach the trap to the boat. Humpbacks can get tangled in the ropes. They also become entangled in fishing nets. The ropes and nets can cut a whale's skin and make it difficult for the whale to feed, mate, and breathe. Special rescue teams are trained to free entangled whales. When they get reports of a trapped whale, they use a small boat to approach it to try to cut the ropes or netting free.

Rescuers attach buoys to the fishing gear to keep a whale near the water's surface. Then, they use long poles with knives attached to cut away rope and netting from the entangled whale. If the ropes have not caused too many injuries, the whale should recover fully.

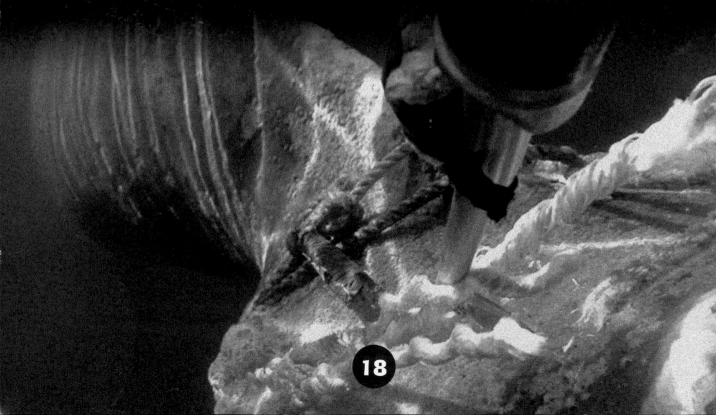

Dead humpback whales occasionally wash up on beaches. This gives scientists a chance to study the creatures. Often, they find ropes or other fishing gear wrapped around the whales. Sometimes, the whale's stomach is full of plastic it has accidentally swallowed in the sea.

A TRAGIC TALE

Spinnaker was a female humpback often sighted in the North Atlantic. In 2006, she became entangled in fishing gear. A team of rescuers freed her. In 2014, Spinnaker was rescued after she was again discovered wound in gear. Less than a year later, the same thing happened. A few weeks later, her dead body was found floating near the shore. Scientists studied her corpse to find out how she died. They discovered rope that was stuck in her mouth and injuries from rope and netting in her throat and neck.

COLLABORATING FOR A CAUSE

Scientists are researching ways to prevent entanglement. At the New England Aquarium in Boston, Massachusetts, experts are testing out new fishing ropes that are designed to have breaking points. These weak sections would allow a whale to break free if it became entangled. Some early research suggests that using bright colors such as red or orange for ropes and nets may also help whales avoid entanglement.

Watch Out for Whales!

Many species share the ocean, including humans and humpbacks. Humpbacks often mate and feed close to the shore. In some places, these areas have high boat traffic. A ship strike occurs when a humpback collides with a boat. Such encounters are dangerous for humpbacks and humans. As boats get bigger and faster, there is a higher risk of strikes. Large vessels use equipment such as **sonar** to detect whales. Slowing down in areas where whales are present also lowers the risk of ship strikes.

Boat propellers can rip large wounds in a whale's skin. Direct hits can be fatal to whales and dangerous to people on board a boat. Wildlife groups such as See a Spout! advise that boaters switch off their engines if they see any whales.

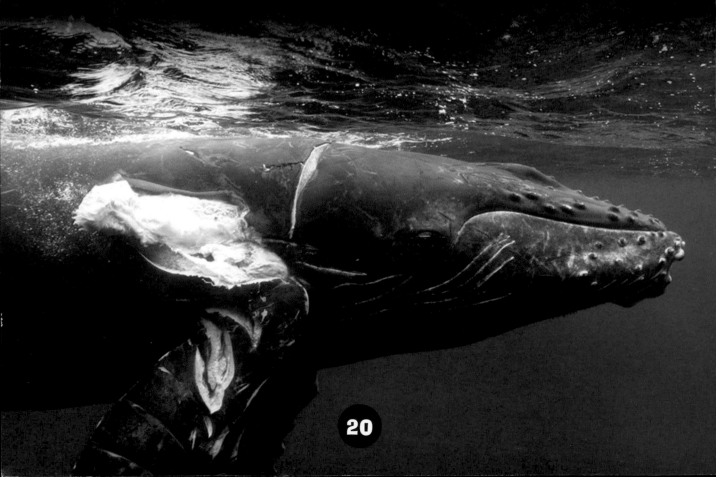

SEE A SPOUT!

A number of voluntary organizations educate people on safety around whales. They cooperate with the National Oceanic and Atmospheric Administration (NOAA) and the Whale and Dolphin Conservation charity to give the best possible advice. The voluntary education program Whale SENSE also offers guidance to whale-watching businesses in the Atlantic and around Alaska. Together, these organizations issue guidelines to any boaters who might come into contact with whales. Their slogan is "See a Spout, Watch Out!" The guidelines advise that if a whale's water spout, tail, or full breeching is spotted, boats should slow down and post a lookout. The lookout should watch to see if the whale surfaces again. Sometimes humpbacks feed or play in large groups, so there may be other whales nearby. Boats should never approach a whale from head on. This disrupts the animal's path and increases the chance of collision. Boats should travel alongside the animal at least 328 feet (100 meters) away. Boaters should also avoid crowding around a whale, which might alarm it. Bubbles may be a sign that a whale is hunting. This means it may surface anywhere unexpectedly.

Environmental Threats

One serious threat to humpback whales comes from global warming, the warming of Earth's temperature. Human activities, such as burning **fossil fuels**, are speeding up global warming, which is warming Earth's oceans. This is affecting the humpbacks' food source.

Krill, the humpback whale's main source of food, feeds on plankton (right). Whales eat plankton too. But plankton lives in cold water. As the ocean warms, the population of plankton will decline. This may cause a fall in krill populations. Feeding grounds for humpbacks will get smaller. Many humpbacks feed in the Gulf of Maine, but it is one of the fastest warming bodies of water on the planet. In 2018, Allied Whale and the Cetos Research Organization began a five-year study of the gulf ecosystem. They want to find out how global warming is affecting the humpback population off the New England coast.

As ocean waters warm and plankton populations decrease, there is less food available for humpbacks. The animals may have to find new areas to feed.

MAKING TOO MUCH NOISE

Noise pollution in the ocean is another problem that humpbacks face. This is sounds made by human activities, such as ship engines. The sounds interfere with a whale's ability to hear. Humpbacks need to hear each other to communicate. Energy exploration is a major source of ocean noise. Many countries look for energy sources, such as oil and natural gas, below the ocean floor. To find these energy sources, ships tow instruments called air guns to help map the ocean floor. These air guns shoot blasts of air into the water every 10 to 15 seconds, causing a loud bang. Sound waves bounce off underwater landforms, and sensors pick up the signals that bounce back, allowing scientists to map the floor and locate resources. Research shows that humpbacks swim away from areas where research blasts are taking place. The noise disrupts activities such as feeding and mating. Scientists continue to study the effects of ocean noise on whales.

Oil rigs are built at the ocean surface to bring up oil from deep below the ocean floor.

Looking Ahead

Humpbacks **migrate** long distances, so in order to track populations researchers use a whale **catalog**. This is a collection of images that show the markings on the underside of a humpback's fluke, or tail fin. Fluke prints are like human fingerprints. They are unique to each whale. A whale is assigned an identification code based on its fluke prints. Scientists use this to track where it travels. Allied Whale is based at the College of the Atlantic in Maine. It organizes the whale catalogs for the North Atlantic and Antarctic populations. The North Atlantic catalog contains images of more than 8,000 individual humpbacks.

Australian scientists use **drones** to study whales from above. This allows them to track whales without causing the animals distress. American researchers flew a drone near a humpback's blowhole to collect water. They studied the spray to see if it contained signs of pollution.

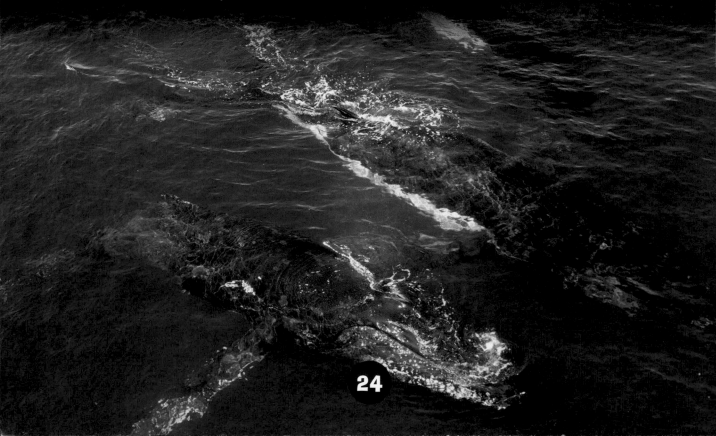

COLLABORATING FOR A CAUSE

A **sanctuary** is a protected space where whale populations are able to recover. In 1979, the IWC worked with national governments to create its first whale sanctuary in the Indian Ocean. In 1994, it set up the Southern Ocean Sanctuary in the waters around Antarctica. This area is an important feeding ground for humpbacks in the Southern Hemisphere. Since 1998, members of the IWC have been trying to set up new sanctuaries in the South Atlantic and South Pacific Oceans. To achieve this, they must collaborate with countries that have coastlines in the region. Many countries and conservation groups, such as Greenpeace and the World Wildlife Federation (WWF), support the creation of these additional sanctuaries. However, nations that want to increase whaling have resisted their creation.

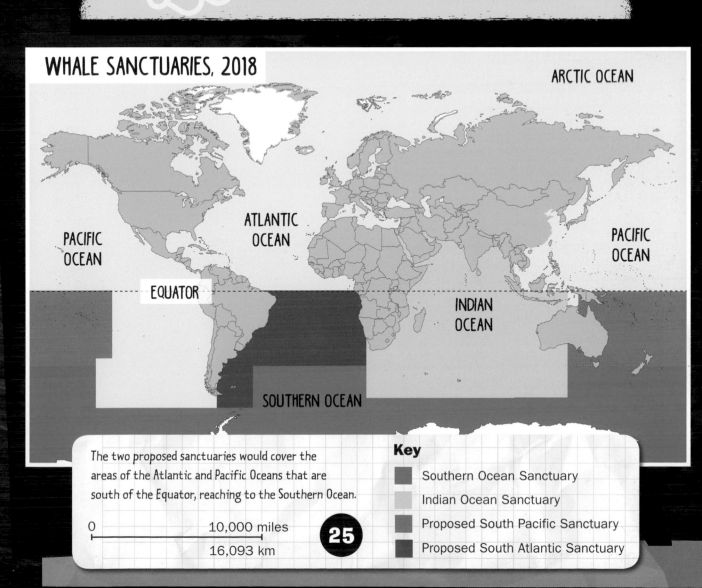

WHALE SANCTUARIES, 2018

ARCTIC OCEAN

PACIFIC OCEAN

ATLANTIC OCEAN

PACIFIC OCEAN

EQUATOR

INDIAN OCEAN

SOUTHERN OCEAN

The two proposed sanctuaries would cover the areas of the Atlantic and Pacific Oceans that are south of the Equator, reaching to the Southern Ocean.

0   10,000 miles
16,093 km

Key

- Southern Ocean Sanctuary
- Indian Ocean Sanctuary
- Proposed South Pacific Sanctuary
- Proposed South Atlantic Sanctuary

Saving Other Species

Bringing the humpback whale back from the brink of extinction is a conservation success story. Many of the dangers that affect humpbacks also threaten other great whales, which is the group of whales that humpbacks belong to. The IWC lists 13 species of great whales. The IUCN classifies seven species as being of Least Concern, five as Endangered, and one as Vulnerable. All the great whales benefit from efforts like those taken to protect humpbacks, such as bans on hunting and steps to reduce noise pollution. The populations of different species are constantly monitored to ensure they remain at healthy levels. However, listing and other efforts to protect whales can have a negative impact on fishers who earn a living on the water. There is still much work to be done to find a way for whales and humans to share the ocean and its resources.

An estimated 300 to 350 North Atlantic right whales, listed as Endangered, still survive. To help protect the whales, the Canadian Department of Fisheries and Oceans does not allow fishers to place nets and traps in areas where North Atlantic right whales live.

About 10,000 southern right whales live in the Southern Ocean around the Antarctic. The IUCN lists the species as being of Least Concern. Nevertheless, the whale is protected by the countries with coasts where it breeds.

The Antarctic minke whale is listed as Near Threatened by the IUCN. The International Whaling Commission estimated in 2012 that there were just 515,000 minke whales.

COLLABORATING FOR A CAUSE

In 2018, the IUCN partnered with Google Earth to create an interactive journey that follows humpbacks on their long annual migration from their breeding grounds to their feeding grounds. The story shares information about threats and conservation efforts that affect all great whales. It also stresses the importance of large-marine ecosystems (LMEs). These are parts of the ocean near coasts where animals such as humpbacks often feed, breed, and raise their young.

Take Action!

It is not only scientists and conservationists who have brought humpbacks back from the brink. Ordinary people have made a difference, too. **Citizen science** projects allow people of all ages to help with research into humpbacks and other whales. People can share data about whale sightings with scientists and organizations. Volunteers in national marine sanctuaries participate in a variety of activities that directly benefit sea creatures, including whale identification and beach cleanups.

In Hawaii, citizen scientists take part in the annual Great Whale Count on the island of Maui. Volunteers count the number of humpback **pods**, individual whales, and calves seen on one day in February. The results give scientists a snapshot of the local population. In 2018, 335 pods were reported, which included 529 whales and 62 calves.

If you get a chance to go whale watching, try and take a photograph of a whale's fluke. You can send the image off to Allied Whale. It might help the group's experts track the whales listed in its whale catalog.

HELPING THE WHALES

The survival of humpbacks, other great whales, and other marine creatures depends on the health of the oceans. Anyone can take actions to help protect the ocean environment.

- Oceans cover more than 70 percent of Earth. Help keep them clean by using environmentally friendly products, recycling, and using less plastic.

- Encourage your family and friends to buy seafood from companies that use environment- and whale-friendly fishing methods. For example, the Seafood Watch program at the Monterey Bay Aquarium provides information about sources of environmentally friendly seafood.

- Speak up and stay informed. Find out all that you can about humpbacks and other whales. Write to your elected representatives to explain why protecting whales is important to everyone. Ask them to support any laws that restrict whaling and protect the marine environment.

Learning More

Books

Eriksson, Ann. *Dive In! Exploring Our Connection with the Ocean.* Orca Book Publishers, 2018.

O'Keefe, Emily. *Humpback Whale. Back from Near Extinction*. Core Library, 2016.

Spilsbury, Louise. *Save the Humpback Whale. Animal SOS!* Windmill Books, 2014.

Young, Karen Romano. *Whale Quest: Working Together to Save Endangered Species.* Twenty-First Century Books, 2018.

On the Web

www.fisheries.noaa.gov/species/humpback-whale
The National Oceanic and Atmospheric Association (NOAA) highlights different humpback whale populations around the world.

wwf.panda.org/our_work/wildlife/profiles/mammals/whales_dolphins/humpback_whale
The World Wildlife Fund provides an overview of humpback whales and conservation efforts to protect them.

ocean.si.edu/ocean-life/marine-mammals/life-after-whale-whale-falls
This short video from the Smithsonian Institution shows the different phases of a whale fall.

https://hawaiihumpbackwhale.noaa.gov/explore/welcome.html
Explore the Hawaiian Islands Humpback Whale National Marine Sanctuary, located off the Hawaiian coast, and learn more about the whales and their habitat.

For videos, activities, and more, enter the access code at the Crabtree Plus website below.

www.crabtreeplus.com/animals-back-brink

Access code: abb37

Glossary

acrobatic Describing a spectacular performance that displays agility

activists People who campaign to bring about change

biologist A scientist who studies living things

blubber The fat of whales and other aquatic animals

breed To mate and have offspring

captivity The state of being kept in one place and not allowed to leave

catalog A group of items, such as images, organized in a system

citizen science The collection of data for scientific surveys by members of the public

conservation The preservation and protection of animals, plants, and natural resources

corsets Tight-fitting garments worn by women to shape their figure

cultivation The deliberate breeding and growing of plants, such as crops

decline Fall in number

drones Unpiloted, remote-controlled aircraft or ships

ecosystems All living and nonliving things in an area, and their relationships with one another

extinct No longer existing

extinction The state at which no living individuals of a species survive

food chain A series of animals, each of which eats the one next to it

fossil fuels Natural fuels such as coal and gas

harpoons Pointed spears used to kill fish and marine animals

hemisphere One of the halves of the globe, divided by the Equator

Indigenous The original people, animals, or plants to live in an area

industry Processing raw materials or manufacturing goods

Inuit Indigenous peoples native to the Arctic regions of Canada, Greenland, and Alaska

krill A small animal with an outer shell that lives in the sea

mammals Animals that feed their young on milk

mate When two animals come together and have offspring

migrate To travel from one place to another at regular times of the year

moratorium A ban on an activity that lasts for a certain period of time

natural resources Useful materials that occur in nature

nutrients Substances that help plants and animals grow by providing food

ocean floor The bottom of the ocean

pectoral fins Describes the fins on or near the chest

pods Groups of the same kind of sea mammals

predators Animals that prey on, or hunt, other animals

sanctuary A protected space for wildlife where hunting is illegal

sonar A device that uses sound waves to locate objects underwater

species A group of similar animals or plants that can breed with one another

subsistence An activity such as farming or hunting that takes place at a minimal level to help people survive

tissue The soft material that forms the parts in a living thing

Index and About the Author

ABOUT THE AUTHOR

Kelly Spence works as a writer and editor of children's books and at a public library. She is an avid reader and animal lover. One of her favorite memories from a trip to the East Coast was watching a pod of humpback whales feed and play in the North Atlantic Ocean—from a safe and whale-friendly distance.